Tattoo

Placement

Theme

Planned Date

Palette

Placement

AF113455

Design

Detail 1

Detail 2

Notes

Tattoo

Placement

Theme

Planned Date

Palette

Placement

Design

Detail 1

Detail 2

Notes

Tattoo

Placement

Theme

Planned Date

Palette

Placement

Design

Detail 1

Detail 2

Notes

Tattoo

Placement

Theme

Planned Date

Palette

Placement

Design

Detail 1

Detail 2

Notes

Tattoo

Placement

Theme

Planned Date

Palette

Placement

Design

Detail 1

Detail 2

Notes

Tattoo

Placement

Theme

Planned Date

Palette

Placement

Design

Detail 1

Detail 2

Notes

Tattoo

Placement

Theme

Planned Date

Palette

Placement

Design

Detail 1

Detail 2

Notes

Tattoo

Placement

Theme

Planned Date

Palette

Placement

Design

Detail 1

Detail 2

Notes

Tattoo

Placement

Theme

Planned Date

Palette

Placement

Design

Detail 1

Detail 2

Notes

Tattoo

Placement

Theme

Planned Date

Palette

Placement

Design

Detail 1

Detail 2

Notes

Tattoo

Placement

Theme

Planned Date

Palette

Placement

Design

Detail 1

Detail 2

Notes

Tattoo

Placement

Theme

Planned Date

Palette

Placement

Design

Detail 1

Detail 2

Notes

Tattoo

Placement

Theme

Planned Date

Palette

Placement

Design

Detail 1

Detail 2

Notes

Tattoo

Placement

Theme

Planned Date

Palette

Placement

Design

Detail 1

Detail 2

Notes

Tattoo

Placement

Theme

Planned Date

Palette

Placement

Design

Detail 1

Detail 2

Notes

Tattoo

Placement

Theme

Planned Date

Palette

Placement

Design

Detail 1

Detail 2

Notes

Tattoo

Placement

Theme

Planned Date

Palette

Placement

Design

Detail 1

Detail 2

Notes

Tattoo

Placement

Theme

Planned Date

Palette

Placement

Design

Detail 1

Detail 2

Notes

Tattoo

Placement

Theme

Planned Date

Palette

Placement

Design

Detail 1

Detail 2

Notes

Tattoo

Placement

Theme

Planned Date

Palette

Placement

Design

Detail 1

Detail 2

Notes

Tattoo

Placement

Theme

Planned Date

Palette

Placement

Design

Detail 1

Detail 2

Notes

Tattoo

Placement

Theme

Planned Date

Palette

Placement

Design

Detail 1

Detail 2

Notes

Tattoo

Placement

Theme

Planned Date

Palette

Placement

Design

Detail 1

Detail 2

Notes

Tattoo

Placement

Theme

Planned Date

Palette

Placement

Design

Detail 1

Detail 2

Notes

Tattoo

Placement

Theme

Planned Date

Palette

Placement

Design

Detail 1

Detail 2

Notes

Tattoo

Placement

Theme

Planned Date

Palette

Placement

Design

Detail 1

Detail 2

Notes

Tattoo

Placement

Theme

Planned Date

Palette

Placement

Design

Detail 1

Detail 2

Notes

Tattoo

Placement

Theme

Planned Date

Palette

Placement

Design

Detail 1

Detail 2

Notes

Tattoo

Placement

Theme

Planned Date

Palette

Placement

Design

Detail 1

Detail 2

Notes

Tattoo

Placement

Theme

Planned Date

Palette

Placement

Design

Detail 1

Detail 2

Notes

Tattoo

Placement

Theme

Planned Date

Palette

Placement

Design

Detail 1

Detail 2

Notes

Tattoo

Placement

Theme

Planned Date

Palette

Placement

Design

Detail 1

Detail 2

Notes

Tattoo

Placement

Theme

Planned Date

Palette

Placement

Design

Detail 1

Detail 2

Notes

Tattoo

Placement

Theme

Planned Date

Palette

Placement

Design

Detail 1

Detail 2

Notes

Tattoo

Placement

Theme

Planned Date

Palette

Placement

Design

Detail 1

Detail 2

Notes

Tattoo

Placement

Theme

Planned Date

Palette

Placement

Design

Detail 1

Detail 2

Notes

Tattoo

Placement

Theme

Planned Date

Palette

Placement

Design

Detail 1

Detail 2

Notes

Tattoo

Placement

Theme

Planned Date

Palette

Placement

Design

Detail 1

Detail 2

Notes

Tattoo

Placement

Theme

Planned Date

Palette

Placement

Design

Detail 1

Detail 2

Notes

Tattoo

Placement

Theme

Planned Date

Palette

Placement

Design

Detail 1

Detail 2

Notes

Tattoo

Placement

Theme

Planned Date

Palette

Placement

Design

Detail 1

Detail 2

Notes

Tattoo

Placement

Theme

Planned Date

Palette

Placement

Design

Detail 1

Detail 2

Notes

Tattoo

Placement

Theme

Planned Date

Palette

Placement

Design

Detail 1

Detail 2

Notes

Tattoo

Placement

Theme

Planned Date

Palette

Placement

Design

Detail 1

Detail 2

Notes

Tattoo

Placement

Theme

Planned Date

Palette

Placement

Design

Detail 1

Detail 2

Notes

Tattoo

Placement

Theme

Planned Date

Palette

Placement

Design

Detail 1

Detail 2

Notes

Tattoo

Placement

Theme

Planned Date

Palette

Placement

Design

Detail 1

Detail 2

Notes

Tattoo

Placement

Theme

Planned Date

Palette

Placement

Design

Detail 1

Detail 2

Notes

Tattoo

Placement

Theme

Planned Date

Palette

Placement

Design

Detail 1

Detail 2

Notes

Tattoo

Placement

Theme

Planned Date

Palette

Placement

Design

Detail 1

Detail 2

Notes

Tattoo

Placement

Theme

Planned Date

Palette

Placement

Design

Detail 1

Detail 2

Notes

Tattoo

Placement

Theme

Planned Date

Palette

Placement

Design

Detail 1

Detail 2

Notes

Tattoo

Placement

Theme

Planned Date

Palette

Placement

Design

Detail 1

Detail 2

Notes

Tattoo

Placement

Theme

Planned Date

Placement

Palette

Design

Detail 1

Detail 2

Notes

Tattoo

Placement

Theme

Planned Date

Palette

Placement

Design

Detail 1

Detail 2

Notes

Tattoo

Placement

Theme

Planned Date

Palette

Placement

Design

Detail 1

Detail 2

Notes

Tattoo

Placement

Theme

Planned Date

Palette

Placement

Design

Detail 1

Detail 2

Notes

Tattoo

Placement

Theme

Planned Date

Palette

Placement

Design

Detail 1

Detail 2

Notes

Tattoo

Placement

Theme

Planned Date

Palette

Placement

Design

Detail 1

Detail 2

Notes

Tattoo

Placement

Theme

Planned Date

Palette

Placement

Design

Detail 1

Detail 2

Notes

Name of Look _____

Evening ○
Daytime ○

Face

Moisturizer

Concealer

Foundation

Highlight/Blush

Eyes

Brows

Eyelid

Liner

Crease

Mascara

Lips

Liner

Lip Color

Gloss

Notes

Name of Look _____

Evening ○
Daytime ○

Face

Moisturizer

_____

Concealer

_____

Foundation

_____

Highlight/Blush

_____

Eyes

Brows

_____

Eyelid

_____

Liner

_____

Crease

_____

Mascara

_____

Lips

Liner

_____

Lip Color

_____

Gloss

_____

Notes

Name of Look _____

Evening ○
Daytime ○

Face

Moisturizer

Concealer

Foundation

Highlight/Blush

Eyes

Brows

Eyelid

Liner

Crease

Mascara

Lips

Liner

Lip Color

Gloss

Notes

Name of Look _____

Evening ○
Daytime ○

Face

Moisturizer

_____

Concealer

_____

Foundation

_____

Highlight/Blush

_____

Eyes

Brows

_____

Eyelid

_____

Liner

_____

Crease

_____

Mascara

_____

Lips

Liner

_____

Lip Color

_____

Gloss

_____

Notes

Name of Look _____

Evening ○
Daytime ○

Face

Moisturizer
_____

Concealer
_____

Foundation
_____

Highlight/Blush
_____

Eyes

Brows
_____

Eyelid
_____

Liner
_____

Crease
_____

Mascara
_____

Lips

Liner
_____

Lip Color
_____

Gloss
_____

Notes

Name of Look _____

Evening ○
Daytime ○

Face
Moisturizer
_____

Concealer
_____

Foundation
_____

Highlight/Blush
_____

Eyes
Brows
_____

Eyelid
_____

Liner
_____

Crease
_____

Mascara
_____

Lips
Liner
_____

Lip Color
_____

Gloss
_____

Notes

Name of Look _____

Evening ○
Daytime ○

Face

Moisturizer

Concealer

Foundation

Highlight/Blush

Eyes

Brows

Eyelid

Liner

Crease

Mascara

Lips

Liner

Lip Color

Gloss

Notes

Name of Look _____

Evening ○
Daytime ○

Face

Moisturizer
_____

Concealer
_____

Foundation
_____

Highlight/Blush
_____

Eyes

Brows
_____

Eyelid
_____

Liner
_____

Crease
_____

Mascara
_____

Lips

Liner
_____

Lip Color
_____

Gloss
_____

Notes

Name of Look _____

Evening ○
Daytime ○

Face

Moisturizer

Concealer

Foundation

Highlight/Blush

Eyes

Brows

Eyelid

Liner

Crease

Mascara

Lips

Liner

Lip Color

Gloss

Notes

Name of Look _____

Evening ○
Daytime ○

Face

Moisturizer
_____

Concealer
_____

Foundation
_____

Highlight/Blush
_____

Eyes

Brows
_____

Eyelid
_____

Liner
_____

Crease
_____

Mascara
_____

Lips

Liner
_____

Lip Color
_____

Gloss
_____

Notes

Name of Look _____

Evening ○
Daytime ○

Face

Moisturizer
_____

Concealer
_____

Foundation
_____

Highlight/Blush
_____

Eyes

Brows
_____

Eyelid
_____

Liner
_____

Crease
_____

Mascara
_____

Lips

Liner
_____

Lip Color
_____

Gloss
_____

Notes

Name of Look _____

Evening ○
Daytime ○

Face
Moisturizer
_____

Concealer
_____

Foundation
_____

Highlight/Blush
_____

Eyes
Brows
_____

Eyelid
_____

Liner
_____

Crease
_____

Mascara
_____

Lips
Liner
_____

Lip Color
_____

Gloss
_____

Notes

Name of Look _____

Evening ○
Daytime ○

Face

Moisturizer

Concealer

Foundation

Highlight/Blush

Eyes

Brows

Eyelid

Liner

Crease

Mascara

Lips

Liner

Lip Color

Gloss

Notes

Name of Look _____

Evening ○
Daytime ○

Face

Moisturizer
_____

Concealer
_____

Foundation
_____

Highlight/Blush
_____

Eyes

Brows
_____

Eyelid
_____

Liner
_____

Crease
_____

Mascara
_____

Lips

Liner
_____

Lip Color
_____

Gloss
_____

Notes

Name of Look _____

Evening ○
Daytime ○

Face
Moisturizer
___

Concealer
___

Foundation
___

Highlight/Blush
___

Eyes
Brows
___

Eyelid
___

Liner
___

Crease
___

Mascara
___

Lips
Liner
___

Lip Color
___

Gloss
___

Notes

Name of Look _____

Evening ○
Daytime ○

Face

Moisturizer

Concealer

Foundation

Highlight/Blush

Eyes

Brows

Eyelid

Liner

Crease

Mascara

Lips

Liner

Lip Color

Gloss

Notes

Name of Look _____

Evening ◯
Daytime ◯

Face
Moisturizer

Concealer

Foundation

Highlight/Blush

Eyes
Brows

Eyelid

Liner

Crease

Mascara

Lips
Liner

Lip Color

Gloss

Notes

Name of Look _____

Evening ○
Daytime ○

Face

Moisturizer

_____

Concealer

_____

Foundation

_____

Highlight/Blush

_____

Eyes

Brows

_____

Eyelid

_____

Liner

_____

Crease

_____

Mascara

_____

Lips

Liner

_____

Lip Color

_____

Gloss

_____

Notes

Name of Look _____

Evening ○
Daytime ○

Face

Moisturizer
_____

Concealer
_____

Foundation
_____

Highlight/Blush
_____

Eyes

Brows
_____

Eyelid
_____

Liner
_____

Crease
_____

Mascara
_____

Lips

Liner
_____

Lip Color
_____

Gloss
_____

Notes

Name of Look _____

Evening ○
Daytime ○

Face

Moisturizer

Concealer

Foundation

Highlight/Blush

Eyes

Brows

Eyelid

Liner

Crease

Mascara

Lips

Liner

Lip Color

Gloss

Notes

Name of Look _____

Evening ○
Daytime ○

Face

Moisturizer
_____

Concealer
_____

Foundation
_____

Highlight/Blush
_____

Eyes

Brows
_____

Eyelid
_____

Liner
_____

Crease
_____

Mascara
_____

Lips

Liner
_____

Lip Color
_____

Gloss
_____

Notes

Name of Look _____

Evening ○
Daytime ○

Face

Moisturizer
_____

Concealer
_____

Foundation
_____

Highlight/Blush
_____

Eyes

Brows
_____

Eyelid
_____

Liner
_____

Crease
_____

Mascara
_____

Lips

Liner
_____

Lip Color
_____

Gloss
_____

Notes

Name of Look _____

Evening ○
Daytime ○

Face
Moisturizer
_____

Concealer
_____

Foundation
_____

Highlight/Blush
_____

Eyes
Brows
_____

Eyelid
_____

Liner
_____

Crease
_____

Mascara
_____

Lips
Liner
_____

Lip Color
_____

Gloss
_____

Notes

Name of Look _____

Evening ○
Daytime ○

Face
Moisturizer

Concealer

Foundation

Highlight/Blush

Eyes
Brows

Eyelid

Liner

Crease

Mascara

Lips
Liner

Lip Color

Gloss

Notes

Name of Look _____

Evening ○
Daytime ○

Face
Moisturizer
_____

Concealer
_____

Foundation
_____

Highlight/Blush
_____

Eyes
Brows
_____

Eyelid
_____

Liner
_____

Crease
_____

Mascara
_____

Lips
Liner
_____

Lip Color
_____

Gloss
_____

Notes

Name of Look _____

Evening ◯
Daytime ◯

Face

Moisturizer

_____

Concealer

_____

Foundation

_____

Highlight/Blush

_____

Eyes

Brows

_____

Eyelid

_____

Liner

_____

Crease

_____

Mascara

_____

Lips

Liner

_____

Lip Color

_____

Gloss

_____

Notes

Name of Look _____

Evening ○
Daytime ○

Face

Moisturizer
_____

Concealer
_____

Foundation
_____

Highlight/Blush
_____

Eyes

Brows
_____

Eyelid
_____

Liner
_____

Crease
_____

Mascara
_____

Lips

Liner
_____

Lip Color
_____

Gloss
_____

Notes

Name of Look _____

Evening ○
Daytime ○

Face

Moisturizer
_____

Concealer
_____

Foundation
_____

Highlight/Blush
_____

Eyes

Brows
_____

Eyelid
_____

Liner
_____

Crease
_____

Mascara
_____

Lips

Liner
_____

Lip Color
_____

Gloss
_____

Notes

Name of Look _____

Evening ○
Daytime ○

Face

Moisturizer

Concealer

Foundation

Highlight/Blush

Eyes

Brows

Eyelid

Liner

Crease

Mascara

Lips

Liner

Lip Color

Gloss

Notes

Name of Look _____

Evening ○
Daytime ○

Face

Moisturizer
_____

Concealer
_____

Foundation
_____

Highlight/Blush
_____

Eyes

Brows
_____

Eyelid
_____

Liner
_____

Crease
_____

Mascara
_____

Lips

Liner
_____

Lip Color
_____

Gloss
_____

Notes

Name of Look _____

Evening ○
Daytime ○

Face
Moisturizer

Concealer

Foundation

Highlight/Blush

Eyes
Brows

Eyelid

Liner

Crease

Mascara

Lips
Liner

Lip Color

Gloss

Notes

Name of Look _____

Evening ○
Daytime ○

Face

Moisturizer

_____

Concealer

_____

Foundation

_____

Highlight/Blush

_____

Eyes

Brows

_____

Eyelid

_____

Liner

_____

Crease

_____

Mascara

_____

Lips

Liner

_____

Lip Color

_____

Gloss

_____

Notes

Name of Look _____

Evening ○
Daytime ○

Face

Moisturizer
_____

Concealer
_____

Foundation
_____

Highlight/Blush
_____

Eyes

Brows
_____

Eyelid
_____

Liner
_____

Crease
_____

Mascara
_____

Lips

Liner
_____

Lip Color
_____

Gloss
_____

Notes

Name of Look _____

Evening ○
Daytime ○

Face

Moisturizer

_____

Concealer

_____

Foundation

_____

Highlight/Blush

_____

Eyes

Brows

_____

Eyelid

_____

Liner

_____

Crease

_____

Mascara

_____

Lips

Liner

_____

Lip Color

_____

Gloss

_____

Notes

Name of Look _____

Evening ○
Daytime ○

Face

Moisturizer

Concealer

Foundation

Highlight/Blush

Eyes

Brows

Eyelid

Liner

Crease

Mascara

Lips

Liner

Lip Color

Gloss

Notes

Name of Look _____

Evening ○
Daytime ○

Face

Moisturizer
_____

Concealer
_____

Foundation
_____

Highlight/Blush
_____

Eyes

Brows
_____

Eyelid
_____

Liner
_____

Crease
_____

Mascara
_____

Lips

Liner
_____

Lip Color
_____

Gloss
_____

Notes

Name of Look _____

Evening ○
Daytime ○

Face

Moisturizer

Concealer

Foundation

Highlight/Blush

Eyes

Brows

Eyelid

Liner

Crease

Mascara

Lips

Liner

Lip Color

Gloss

Notes

Name of Look _____

Evening ○
Daytime ○

Face

Moisturizer
_____

Concealer
_____

Foundation
_____

Highlight/Blush
_____

Eyes

Brows
_____

Eyelid
_____

Liner
_____

Crease
_____

Mascara
_____

Lips

Liner
_____

Lip Color
_____

Gloss
_____

Notes

Name of Look _____

Evening ○
Daytime ○

Face

Moisturizer
_____

Concealer
_____

Foundation
_____

Highlight/Blush
_____

Eyes

Brows
_____

Eyelid
_____

Liner
_____

Crease
_____

Mascara
_____

Lips

Liner
_____

Lip Color
_____

Gloss
_____

Notes

Name of Look _____

Evening ○
Daytime ○

Face
Moisturizer
_____

Concealer
_____

Foundation
_____

Highlight/Blush
_____

Eyes
Brows
_____

Eyelid
_____

Liner
_____

Crease
_____

Mascara
_____

Lips
Liner
_____

Lip Color
_____

Gloss
_____

Notes

Name of Look _____

Evening ○
Daytime ○

Face

Moisturizer

Concealer

Foundation

Highlight/Blush

Eyes

Brows

Eyelid

Liner

Crease

Mascara

Lips

Liner

Lip Color

Gloss

Notes

Name of Look _____

Evening ○
Daytime ○

Face
Moisturizer
_____

Concealer
_____

Foundation
_____

Highlight/Blush
_____

Eyes
Brows
_____

Eyelid
_____

Liner
_____

Crease
_____

Mascara
_____

Lips
Liner
_____

Lip Color
_____

Gloss
_____

Notes

Name of Look _____

Evening ○
Daytime ○

Face

Moisturizer

Concealer

Foundation

Highlight/Blush

Eyes

Brows

Eyelid

Liner

Crease

Mascara

Lips

Liner

Lip Color

Gloss

Notes

Name of Look _____

Evening ◯
Daytime ◯

Face
Moisturizer

Concealer

Foundation

Highlight/Blush

Eyes
Brows

Eyelid

Liner

Crease

Mascara

Lips
Liner

Lip Color

Gloss

Notes

Name of Look _____

Evening ◯
Daytime ◯

Face

Moisturizer

Concealer

Foundation

Highlight/Blush

Eyes

Brows

Eyelid

Liner

Crease

Mascara

Lips

Liner

Lip Color

Gloss

Notes

Name of Look _____

Evening ○
Daytime ○

Face
Moisturizer
_____

Concealer
_____

Foundation
_____

Highlight/Blush
_____

Eyes
Brows
_____

Eyelid
_____

Liner
_____

Crease
_____

Mascara
_____

Lips
Liner
_____

Lip Color
_____

Gloss
_____

Notes

Name of Look _____

Evening ○
Daytime ○

Face

Moisturizer
_____

Concealer
_____

Foundation
_____

Highlight/Blush
_____

Eyes

Brows
_____

Eyelid
_____

Liner
_____

Crease
_____

Mascara
_____

Lips

Liner
_____

Lip Color
_____

Gloss
_____

Notes

Name of Look _____

Evening ○
Daytime ○

Face
Moisturizer
_____

Concealer
_____

Foundation
_____

Highlight/Blush
_____

Eyes
Brows
_____

Eyelid
_____

Liner
_____

Crease
_____

Mascara
_____

Lips
Liner
_____

Lip Color
_____

Gloss
_____

Notes

Name of Look _____

Evening ◯
Daytime ◯

Face

Moisturizer

Concealer

Foundation

Highlight/Blush

Eyes

Brows

Eyelid

Liner

Crease

Mascara

Lips

Liner

Lip Color

Gloss

Notes

Name of Look _____

Evening ⃝
Daytime ⃝

Face

Moisturizer

_____

Concealer

_____

Foundation

_____

Highlight/Blush

_____

Eyes

Brows

_____

Eyelid

_____

Liner

_____

Crease

_____

Mascara

_____

Lips

Liner

_____

Lip Color

_____

Gloss

_____

Notes

Name of Look _____

Evening ○
Daytime ○

Face

Moisturizer
_____

Concealer
_____

Foundation
_____

Highlight/Blush
_____

Eyes

Brows
_____

Eyelid
_____

Liner
_____

Crease
_____

Mascara
_____

Lips

Liner
_____

Lip Color
_____

Gloss
_____

Notes

Name of Look _____

Evening ○
Daytime ○

Face

Moisturizer
_____

Concealer
_____

Foundation
_____

Highlight/Blush
_____

Eyes

Brows
_____

Eyelid
_____

Liner
_____

Crease
_____

Mascara
_____

Lips

Liner
_____

Lip Color
_____

Gloss
_____

Notes

Name of Look _____

Evening ○
Daytime ○

Face

Moisturizer
_____

Concealer
_____

Foundation
_____

Highlight/Blush
_____

Eyes

Brows
_____

Eyelid
_____

Liner
_____

Crease
_____

Mascara
_____

Lips

Liner
_____

Lip Color
_____

Gloss
_____

Notes

Name of Look _____

Evening ○
Daytime ○

Face
Moisturizer
_____

Concealer
_____

Foundation
_____

Highlight/Blush
_____

Eyes
Brows
_____

Eyelid
_____

Liner
_____

Crease
_____

Mascara
_____

Lips
Liner
_____

Lip Color
_____

Gloss
_____

Notes

Name of Look _____

Evening ○
Daytime ○

Face

Moisturizer

Concealer

Foundation

Highlight/Blush

Eyes

Brows

Eyelid

Liner

Crease

Mascara

Lips

Liner

Lip Color

Gloss

Notes

Name of Look _____

Evening ◯
Daytime ◯

Face
Moisturizer
_____

Concealer
_____

Foundation
_____

Highlight/Blush
_____

Eyes
Brows
_____

Eyelid
_____

Liner
_____

Crease
_____

Mascara
_____

Lips
Liner
_____

Lip Color
_____

Gloss
_____

Notes

Name of Look _____

Evening ○
Daytime ○

Face

Moisturizer

Concealer

Foundation

Highlight/Blush

Eyes

Brows

Eyelid

Liner

Crease

Mascara

Lips

Liner

Lip Color

Gloss

Notes

Name of Look _____

Evening ○
Daytime ○

Face

Moisturizer
_____

Concealer
_____

Foundation
_____

Highlight/Blush
_____

Eyes

Brows
_____

Eyelid
_____

Liner
_____

Crease
_____

Mascara
_____

Lips

Liner
_____

Lip Color
_____

Gloss
_____

Notes

Name of Look _____

Evening ○
Daytime ○

Face

Moisturizer

Concealer

Foundation

Highlight/Blush

Eyes

Brows

Eyelid

Liner

Crease

Mascara

Lips

Liner

Lip Color

Gloss

Notes

Name of Look _____

Evening ○
Daytime ○

Face

Moisturizer
_____

Concealer
_____

Foundation
_____

Highlight/Blush
_____

Eyes

Brows
_____

Eyelid
_____

Liner
_____

Crease
_____

Mascara
_____

Lips

Liner
_____

Lip Color
_____

Gloss
_____

Notes

www.ingramcontent.com/pod-product-compliance
Lightning Source LLC
LaVergne TN
LVHW012117070526
838202LV00056B/5759